© 2015 Poems by Anthony Lawrence
© 2015 Photographs by Jaime Fleming
All rights reserved.
ISBN: 0692409866

, said the kid with the broken halo

written by a. s. lawrence
photographs by j. l. fleming

for my sister, who can still find the humor in a password and those who know what it means to have a party on the inside.

for stella

"A poem begins as a lump in the throat, a sense of wrong, a homesickness, a lovesickness. It finds the thought and the thought finds the words."

- Robert Frost

Contents

across the universe..9

luminescence...10

cc: cupid..12

he said, she said..13

confession...14

brown-eyed evening primrose..16

autumn..18

hopeless mumbo jumbo...20

vision..22

i put words on a string and burned the edges.......................25

standard issue..29

the tyranny of want...30

the manipulation of mother nature.......................................31

the fall of man...33

gravedigger..35

tiny boats and baptisms..36

eternal and ephemeral..37

with a sting in the tail..38

an audiobook in one breath..41

throw yourself down...42

wild things..43

blue prints..44

down with unsavory boys...46

window seat...48

catharsis..49

the new commandment..50

object-relations..51

,said the kid with the broken halo...52

across the universe

_____

this poem was born of rain and bare feet
God is in the rain
and of matching shoes
stuffed animals and piggy banks
of sleeping dogs on a porch in jamaica and french toast at hue
atop the bank of america building inside a cup of soup
born of wicked and fela
in the pit of a mango
of fireworks, tears, cherry blossoms, and graffiti
this poem was born of the elements born of us
and across the universe we stretch

luminescence
_____

an unexpected incident
a theft of the heart
snow flurries tickle my face
God and mother nature share a piragua
i form a cradle with my hands intending to taste heaven
instead i catch a dripping sunset
it is lukewarm
i put it in my pocket and wait for flowers to grow
then cut two from their stems
and feed them to the butterflies in my belly
i will give the rest to the girl from my dreams
she is daughter to the sum of all things
i am the astronomer who recognizes that her beauty
was composed from the secrets of galaxies
her heart beats a symphony
she can feel the music in her throat
this is the party that i must attend
i breathe deep and ask her to dance
she smiles and offers her hand
it is soft like a whisper

cc: cupid
_____

i am the arrow
she was born of apple seeds
i say you, shoot straight

he said, she said
_____

he said, "the truth will leave you exposed.
lying in wait. naked for all to see. frozen, staring at a mirage of what might have been, what could be."

she said, "the truth is sharp so that it can penetrate the spirit, and it cuts at both ends. it strips us bare so that our genuine selves are not obstructed when they exit the wound. your suffocation is the reason you lie in wait, but the truth will move you a breath closer to the gardener you are meant to be. so, ignore that little fish bone caught in your throat and empty yourself into me."

confession
_____

listen carefully
you'll hear the city speaking
i dreamt of you once

brown-eyed evening primrose
___

intoxicated from shots of thunder,
a brown-eyed evening primrose.
the anguish in her voice crashes against unsuspecting drums,
forcing his way beneath the skirt of evening,
i wonder if he found water in her desert.
did the song of wild coyotes force its way from her throat?
the thought makes me vomit.
vultures claw their way from my mouth.
born from the tornado in my belly,
their onyx feathers slicked from amniotic fluid,
they wait purposefully,
with moonlight illuminating my pane
i dream of his fee,
desert flowers do not come cheap.
apologetically, she lends her suffering to me
so that it might be repurposed into unscathed verse,
but you are not fooled by the calmness of my stroke,
there is a putridness about these curves
and storm clouds loom overhead.

autumn
_____

a falling leaf
unpredictable pattern
the cycle of life

hopeless mumbo jumbo
_____

3

ashes to ashes.
i will not ascend from the ashes, as i am so accustomed to being
abased that my ambition has been arrested.
bound and beaten,
bloodied and bundled in black
cloth to compensate for my color,
confusing those claiming unfamiliarity with the carnival of cane.
doubt, the destroyer of dreams,
easily eradicates enthusiasm as if it were a silken thread,
exchanging it for
frustration that becomes fixated on fledgling faces until finally it
fulminates into one phosphorescent flash;
fireworks of failure.

2

generations of genocide generate
hereditary hate, while
inequality intertwined with ignorance acts as an interlude to unjust
judgments in Jena.
karma for us?
Katrina Killed my Kin in new orleans,
and they did the same thing down in mississippi.
ain't no good karma for us!
look at my lineage.
they learned languages of labor, lashings, and lynchings.
still, while lacking liberty's illumination, they were not lost in
life's labyrinth,
they just learned to lead in the dark.
melancholy memories of masters and minstrels have managed
to manifest in the minds of the
nameless negro

nurturing a never-ending narcosis of thought.
our own oppression's have become omnipresent,
overshadowing our offspring.
partial promises of parity pacify a percentage of our people,
while pursuits of pleasure have preoccupied the rest.
paranoia of the polls preserve political philosophies that portray us as a problem.
quickly one must question the quality of equality and must not do so quietly for fear of quarantine.
relapse and remember the retrospective voices of the Renaissance…in Harlem.
surrender to their sonnets and their stories of struggle and solace.
seek not to shelter your sanity from their sullen symphonies.
let them seep into your soul and shatter a selfish silence,
steal the sound from
thunder and translate it into a temporal tongue,
then telegraph the Timekeeper the theft is only temporary.
use it to unify the unmotivated and the uneducated until the umbra of unity becomes ubiquitous.
only then can we usurp the power of the universe.

1

vacate acts of ventriloquism.
vow to be so vehement when verbalizing verses that the very sound of your voice causes vibrations in water.
write the words that come without warning to ward off weakness and replenish withered spirits,
write the words that will others to stop wasting time waiting with crossed fingers,
recite the words that urge us to wager on ourselves,
for when we realize our worth,
our excellence is exposed, no need for an X-ray.
how easy it becomes then to organize and exodus from the excuses of yesterday.

Zero

vision
_____

dancing on concrete
favors sparklers on the Fourth
city lights and rain

i put words on a string and burned the edges

I.

capitalism
materialism
social darwinism

"affluenza"

greed
envy
chicago
mississippi

racism
classism
sexism

"the american dream"

levy
broke
float
hope

II.

langston
pablo
common
q-tip
mos def
kanye
black thought
lupe

talib
sam
lauryn
pharoahe
poet
k.r.i.t.
odetta

III.

weary, weary, weary early in de morn,
mondays are meshed with tuesdays
and the week with the whole year.
in search of brighter days, i ride through the maze of the madness,
struggle is my address,
hip hop came, the ghetto copped the soundtrack,
working class poor, better keep your alarm clock set, streets too loud to ever hear freedom ring.
having money's not everything, not having it is,
i'm a have not, grandma's grandma suffered.

let's pray for 'em
let the beat play for 'em
put the trouble on display for 'em

work 'till we break our back and you hear the crack of the bone.
there been times i thought i couldn't last for long.
though i had to turn my back on what got you paid,
i couldn't see i had the hood on me like abu ghraib.
survival of the fittest with hope in the eye.
yet, i'm about to change their focus, from the richest to the brokest, i'll write an opus to reverse the hypnosis,
my ministry will leave the industry in a tailspin,
time to push the envelope like u.s. mailmen,
fuck a sword, i told the man in the mirror to go and fetch an ink pen,
but he smiled and said, "son, i can do you one better."
then removed a pocket knife and cut me down from my oppressor.

iv.

oh freedom,
oh freedom,
oh freedom over me,
and before i'd be a slave,
i'll be buried in my grave
and go home to my Lord and be free.

the tyranny of want
___

someday little sister there will be wars fought inside you,
the drummers and buglers will call,
the march of infantry men will cause you to twist up inside,
and from the stabs of bayonets,
you will toss and turn in your fort of blankets and sheets,
there will be many casualties
and the earth will be peeled naked,
such is the fate of he who yearns for the romanticized notions
that tongues have long destroyed,
but do not be discouraged
the fighting doesn't last forever,
and afterward, you'll have a purple heart
to show for your heroism.

standard issue
_____

it feels
strange,
your life
around my neck,
flimsy,
dangling
from its chain
like a custom accessory,
but don't worry,
i keep it close to me,
no one deserves to lose their life
twice.

the manipulation of mother nature
___

flesh melds with bamboo
soon he plucks fish from her veins
like grapes from a vine

the fall of man
_____

then the Lord formed a man from the dust of the ground and breathed
into his nostrils the breath of life,
and the man became a living being,
and was like blown glass,
and was whole and
beautiful,
and was fashioned a great cathedral with full processional doors,
two in number,
ornate rose windows just beneath each brow,
and an impressive sculptural group as its central feature, just south of
his nave.

then the Lord made a woman from a pew that was taken out of the
man,
and He brought her to him,
and she, without knowing, scratched the raw of his lust
when she gave to him who was with her
and he ate,
for his vision was made clear
and he saw that woman was pleasing,
an echo of his inner beauty,
and man was fascinated with his private parts,
she became as ripened fruit and in him grew a considerable hunger,
asphyxiating his knowledge.

once again the serpent spoke to man,
and his vision was made narrow,
and he reached out his hand to grasp at her limbs,
but was struck down by the flaming sword
and fell upon his belly,
and was like blown glass,
scattered amongst the soil like seeds,
countless shards, serrated and piercing,

salvageable still, in the hands of a lover,
this is why she ends her speech with, "despite what you may think, you are a great guy,"
she is aware that i was whole once,
and
beautiful.

gravedigger
_____

grab my journal from the bookshelf,
then look in my desk where i keep my pens
and hand me a shovel,
got some pain needs buryin'.
no similes gonna make me smile,
no sir,
i ain't got time to think of clever metaphors,
i know exactly how deep it needs to be.
besides, i got to get it done before them tears start to fall,
not wise to dig in the rain.

tiny boats and baptisms
_____

a man walks past carrying a saw,
there is the sound of steel on metal,
then metal on linoleum,
rain on tin,
a hammer flirting with wood,
reminiscent of a playground crush,
a voice on a radio warns of a leaking elevator shaft,
a woman approaches and asks to be pointed in the direction of the restroom,
i tell her i'm not familiar with the building,
but point in the direction of an exit sign,
i am stationary,
held by the mundane calmness of life inside an aquarium,
tucked in the folds of harsh incandescent lighting,
measuring the intensity of the royal blue tang in units of envy,
she says i am foolish for leaving my umbrella on a day when tiny boats might not stay tethered to their docks,
and for thinking kerosene will wash off with rain water,
but recognizes that i am in need of relief
and swims in the direction of an exit sign.

eternal and ephemeral
_____

I.

i am sure that neither death nor life,
nor angels, nor rulers,
nor things present nor things to come,
nor powers, nor height, nor depth,
nor anything else in all creation will be able to separate us…

II.

how much do i love you?
perhaps i will take photographs of infinity
and have them infinitely delivered,
hopefully then you will get the picture.

III.

this is just to say,
i apologize for distorting the inner you
and holding you hostage four years.

IV.

step right up! step right up!
twenty will get you forty and forty will get you eighty!
keep your eyes on the hands and not the man.
you sir, can you find the love?

V.

"you are the prettiest thing i've seen in real life,"
said the fly to the spider.

with a sting in the tail
_____

her face puts my mind to sleep,
self-preservation to combat the dissonance,
but she'd sooner see me implode
than be my lullaby from a distance.

throw yourself down
_____

there she is,
grinning her Samedi grin,
looking closely i can see the heat radiating from her skin,
much like staring down a stretch of desert highway in the dead of summer with no cars to obstruct my view,
residual footprints of ash revealed each time her feet are lifted,
even from this distance
i begin to feel a tingle in my wings
and notice a slight discoloration of my scales,
closer now,
with her soot colored hair and scarlet stained nails,
grinning her Samedi grin,
i have no doubt that she can smell the desire to partake of the serpent's fruit seeping from my skin,
like alcohol exiting the pores of a drunkard the morning after,
i am highly flammable and she is wildfire.

an audiobook in one breath
_____

exiting the bus,
i heard her say,
"see, that's why i don't fuck with them type of niggas!"
aimed at my back, her words left me gasping for air.
with one breath she spoke a couple hundred pages.

wild things
_____

soon we will visit the place where the wild things are

and we will pretend that it is Rome…

for now let us continue watching the wild flowers grow

blue prints
_____

there was a time when my sister and i transformed hallways into arenas
using empty skoal cans and cheap dollar store brooms,
taught silver dollar stones to play hopscotch on the belly of shallow creeks,
and drank honeysuckle cocktails beneath the mississippi sun,
back when saturday was still saturday and there was no need to
negotiate time to watch morning cartoons,
and the phrase "self-care" did not exist in our lexicon,
before book fairs were replaced by literature reviews
and curiosities needed the approval of institutional review boards,
before orange juice became tall hazelnut macchiatos with soy no whip
and glitter multicolored pens were traded in for black or blue ink,
before roller blades and bike paths turned into danskos and IVs,
there was a time when our footprints resembled kaleidoscopes
and we were secure in our freedom to chase tomorrow,
before our skin became a polished metallic and we discovered the
blueprints for monotony.

down with unsavory boys
_____

you hold me as if you've done this before,
carefully angled away from your face.
either you are of the mind that believes there is too much intimacy in a kiss for it to be given away haphazardly,
or you have mastered many tongues
and are able to decipher the flicker behind my iris.
it says there is an intense heat inside me waiting to be ignited
that will burn brightly…steadily,
causing your face to glow a kind of reddish-orange,
similar to the end of a burning cigarette
being pulled by the pursed lips of an addict.
like it, i too will be satisfying,
but short-lived,
burning long enough that a passerby might see
that we are alive.

window seat
_____

i am curious as to where they will end,
you'd never think so,
but shooting stars and speeding headlights
look the same to a dreamer.

catharsis
_____

before it revealed itself
i sat facing her,
full from melancholy that has long since settled
at the pit of the stomach,
sifting through a collection of memories,
like old pennies,
i am confronted with an unwavering scripture.

beneath the flesh and bone,
inside the cavities and chambers and sinews of men
lies the secret word for life,
a whisper of syllables to divorce us from all other things
born of ash and dust,
inside this room with no windows,
where we come to re-interpret what has been scribbled on the pages of
a once closed book,
i realize that our thousand different names are but pseudonyms,
as we are all scribes seeking to master the art of storytelling.

"take up your lantern,"
"travel up through the healing spirals
and seat yourself next to your shadow,"
"and break bread,"
these are the things my eyes say.
afterward,
for the last ten minutes,
we sat,
together,
unable to control the laughter of our soul.

the new commandment
_____

beloved, let us love one another wholly,
like bursts of sunlight upon blades of grass.
these are the instructions written on the quadrants of her body.

"this is the new commandment He has given us,"
her shoulder says to my fingers.
"and whoever loves has been born of Him,"
my fingers say to her ribs.

we carry on in this way for some time.
in the darkness
we lie almost motionless,
listening intently as God gives his lecture.

object-relations
_____

ghosts…transient dreams
wavering dandelion
sweeps the dust from porch

,said the kid with the broken halo
_____

forgive me for stirring the pot
and for stepping on toes,
for letting years slip through the space between the minutes,
losing happy endings in pursuit of poetry,
this poem was born of insecurity and uncertainty,
selfishness and hedonism,
unfamiliar spines housing old notes between linen pages,
make-shift bookmarks privately selecting the combination of words that most resonate with the soul,
born of the realization that there have been too many
~~love~~ lust poems,
forgive me,
for running around haphazardly
with a bulge in my pants
made from the random assortment of ink pens
that have gathered in my pockets.

www.ingramcontent.com/pod-product-compliance
Lightning Source LLC
Chambersburg PA
CBHW041757040426
42446CB00005B/238